How to Draw
Cute Stuff
AROUND
THE WORLD

This book belongs to:

....

....

How to Draw
Cute Stuff
AROUND
THE WORLD

Angela Nguyen

union
square
kids

NEW YORK

union
square
kids

NEW YORK

UNION SQUARE KIDS and the distinctive Union
Square Kids logo are trademarks of Union
Square & Co., LLC.

Union Square & Co., LLC., is a subsidiary of
Sterling Publishing Co., Inc.

© 2021 Quarto Publishing plc

First Sterling edition published in 2021

ISBN 978-1-4549-4371-6

For information about custom editions, special
sales, and premium purchases, please contact
specialsales@unionsquareandco.com.

Manufactured in Singapore

Lot #:
2 4 6 8 10 9 7 5 3
09/22

unionsquareandco.com

FSC
www.fsc.org

MIX
Paper from
responsible sources
FSC™ C007207

CONTENTS

Hi there, my name is Angela!

I'm an artist who specializes in drawing cute things, from people, to animals, to objects, and even buildings! Anything and everything can be transformed into cuteness; and I'm going to show you how!

I love to travel to learn about other cultures and cities. Discovering new places is also a form of inspiration for me. I'll take you with me around the world so we can draw cute things and places together. In this book, I will share with you some of my favorite places, so let's go!

Yours truly, Angela Nguyen

To you, dear reader

Your street

Your town

Your country . . .

. . . wherever you are in the world!

OUR WORLD JOURNEY

CANADA
PAGE 22

UNITED STATES OF AMERICA
PAGE 26

3 MEXICO
PAGE 34

4 BRAZIL
PAGE 38

5 PERU
PAGE 42

6 CHILE
PAGE 46

7 SOUTH AFRICA
PAGE 50

8 ETHIOPIA
PAGE 56

9 EGYPT
PAGE 58

10 MOROCCO
PAGE 62

11 SPAIN
PAGE 66

12 ITALY
PAGE 68

13 FRANCE
PAGE 70

14 NETHERLANDS
PAGE 74

Your journey starts here

15 UNITED KINGDOM PAGE 76

16 NORDICS PAGE 80

17 HUNGARY PAGE 84

18 RUSSIA PAGE 86

19 SOUTH KOREA PAGE 90

20 JAPAN PAGE 94

21 TAIWAN PAGE 98

22 CHINA PAGE 100

23 INDIA PAGE 108

24 VIETNAM PAGE 112

25 AUSTRALIA PAGE 118

26 NEW ZEALAND PAGE 124

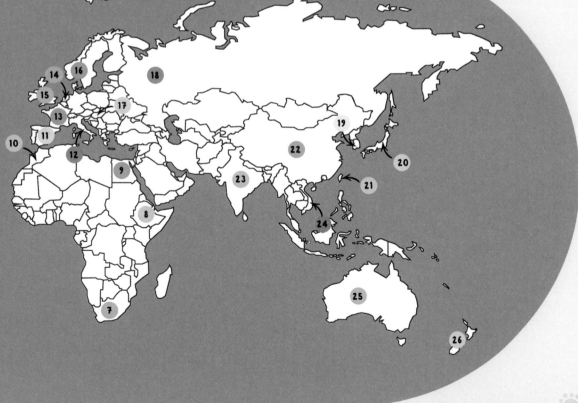

Our world journey

Chapter 1

PACK YOUR BAGS

Before your drawing journey begins, find out about the tools you're going to use on your trip. There are some useful drawing tips included in this chapter, too. Look through these pages and you will have all you need for your world tour.

TOOLS AND SURFACES

You don't need fancy or special tools to draw cute art. There are many types of tools you can use, but the key thing to remember is to choose something that you are comfortable with. Here are some of my favorite tools.

Pencils are perfect for starting out.

PENCILS
Pencils are ideal for sketching and creating fun textures. Pencil marks are also easy to erase if you make any mistakes.

Colored pencils are also great for sketching. Try not to drop colored pencils because the lead inside will break.

SURFACES
You don't need special paper; any kind of drawing surface is fine. If you want to keep all your drawings together, use a sketchbook or notepad.

There's no going back with a pen.

Sharpies define lines.

Be bold with a marker.

MARKERS
Markers are perfect for bold lines and bright colors. I have some markers in my art studio that are thick and create beautiful strokes.

Play with colors, and combine them.

CRAYONS
If you're going to be doing a lot of coloring, crayons can be a fun tool to play with. They make interesting textures.

PENS
These are my favorite! Pens are great when you want a thin stroke. You can get precise drawings, like small paws or little whiskers.

START WITH SHAPES

The world is full of amazing things that you can draw using just a few basic shapes.

The three you know

Let's start with a circle, a triangle, and a square. Each shape can be drawn longer, skinnier, fatter, larger, or smaller to create other shapes.

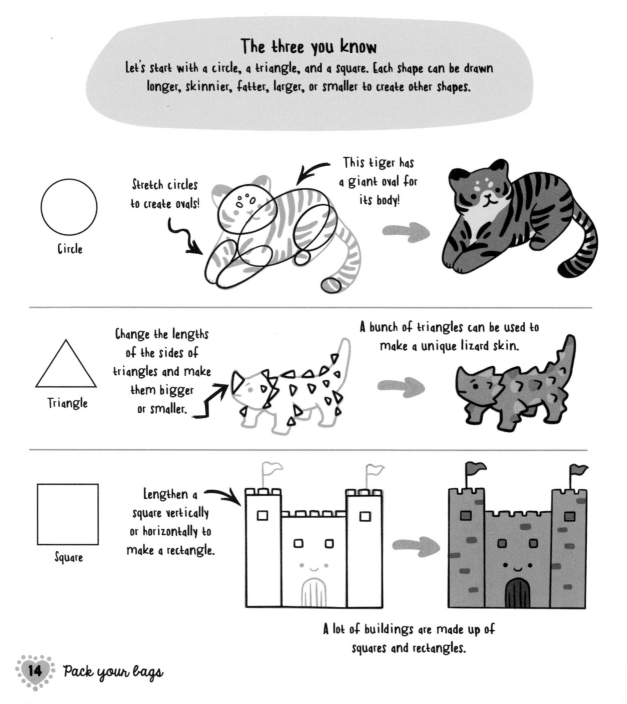

Circle

Stretch circles to create ovals!

This tiger has a giant oval for its body!

Triangle

Change the lengths of the sides of triangles and make them bigger or smaller.

A bunch of triangles can be used to make a unique lizard skin.

Square

Lengthen a square vertically or horizontally to make a rectangle.

A lot of buildings are made up of squares and rectangles.

Special shapes

Now let's look at three special shapes that will come in handy.

Blob

A blob is drawn using squiggly lines.

Squiggly blobs make up the foliage of a Japanese bonsai tree.

Jelly bean

Check out this big jelly bean.

The jelly-bean shape is my favorite to draw! It is mostly used for the bodies of animals.

Gumdrop

You can make some fun creatures with this shape.

Gumdrops are a good shape to try out.

FROM SHAPES TO BASES

Every drawing has a base. The base is a combination of the main shapes that make up your drawing.

Drawing the base
Drawings of animals, objects, buildings, even people, start with a base. The base helps you set up your drawing.

This is the base of a person (me), which is made up of a circle, rectangles, and a gumdrop.

Circle

Gumdrop

Rectangles

Once you have your base, you can add details.

Circle

Triangles

Oval

The base of this dog is made up of a circle, an oval, rectangles, and triangles.

Rectangles

Drawing step by step

As we travel through the countries and learn about their culture, I will show you how to draw step by step using shapes and bases. The gray lines indicate the first steps, then darker lines show what to draw next.

Make a pencil sketch of the base—you will erase some of these lines later. This base is made up of a circle and a gumdrop.

Add rectangles for the arms and legs, a semicircle ear, and two dots for eyes, plus a cute smile of course.

Erase the lines you don't need!

These lines have been erased.

Next, draw the hands, feet, and hair.

Erase those parts of the head that are covered by the hair.

Add details like the jacket and shoes.

Have fun coloring in the shapes!

KEEP IT CUTE

Now that you know the basics of drawing with shapes and bases, here are some extra, easy-to-use tips to help you make sure what you draw is always cute.

Simplify

The most important step when making cute drawings is to simplify what you draw by using less detail. Keep to the basic shapes so your drawing can focus on being cute.

Notice the difference between a realistic and a cute drawing of the same dog. Simpler shapes and less detail are key.

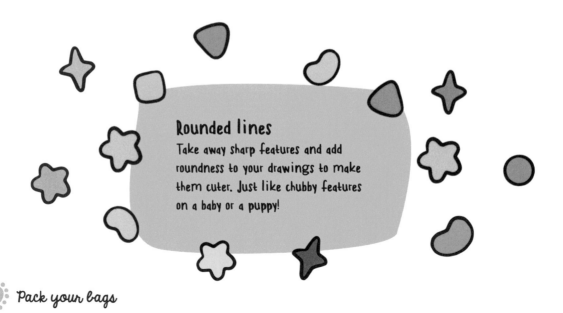

Rounded lines

Take away sharp features and add roundness to your drawings to make them cuter. Just like chubby features on a baby or a puppy!

Faces

Add a cute face to anything you draw to transform it into an adorable character!

Colors

Dark and dull colors make your drawing look very serious. Light, pastel, or bright colors give cute drawings a soft touch.

Add a face to the ice cream . . .

. . . or the cone

Sharp lines

Lots of detail

This is the Sydney Opera House in Australia. I drew it using lots of lines and details.

We can make it cuter by simplifying the shapes and rounding the lines. There are no complicated details, but there is a face, and musical notes have been added!

Rounded lines

Cute face

Chapter 2

AROUND THE WORLD

Your world tour starts in the far north and ends in the far south, and you'll visit lots of exciting countries in between. You'll find out a little about each country's customs, foods, animals, landmarks, transport, costumes, and more.

Make sure you've got your paper, pencils, or other marking tools, and let's draw cute things while we travel.

CANADA

Canada is a huge country with incredible animals and wintry landscapes. You'll also find amazing cities like Toronto and Vancouver; they are so close to the landscapes that you can see the mountains behind the skyscrapers.

The Canadian flag

A happy beaver with happy paws.

Canada has lots of amazing animals, including wolves, mountain lions, beavers, and American buffalo. In the north, you'll find black bears, moose, and even reindeer.

Japadog is a Japanese style hot dog that originated in Vancouver.

Maple syrup is made with sap from maple trees.

Angry eyebrows make tough wolves cute.

Maple leaf

For the maple leaf, start with a circle.

Next, add three large leaf sections evenly around the circle. Don't forget to add a stalk!

Keep adding smaller leaf sections in between the large ones you drew.

Maple leaves change color each season. Color your leaves red for the fall or make them green for the spring!

Snow sports

In Canada, a tuque is a type of warm hat. Grab a tuque and some gloves to go skating!

Draw faces on the hockey stick and puck for extra cuteness.

Canada gets lots of snow, so ice hockey and ice skating are very popular.

Continue drawing in horns for the antlers.

The moose is made up of round shapes. I like to start with the small circular head, and then draw the large oval body.

Add in details like the hanging fur below the neck.

The fur hanging from a moose's neck is called a dewlap.

Once you have added more details to your moose, erase the pencil lines.

When coloring the moose, you will need three colors: a light tan for the antlers, a brown for the fur, and a darker brown for the hooves.

Like for most animals, start with a small round head and a large oval body.

Add rectangular limbs, a curved triangular tail, and triangle ears.

Add cute eyebrows.

For the last part of the line art, add in fur around the tail, back, ears, and neck. Don't forget the face!

Play around with colors! Notice how I use four different shades of brown to layer the fur.

Beaver

Did you know that the beaver is Canada's largest rodent? It has a round face and body, which makes it look cuddly.

The feet look like maple leaves. Imagine drawing three petals.

UNITED STATES OF AMERICA

The American flag

The United States of America covers a large part of North America. It's divided into 50 different states, each with their own special foods, scenery, culture, and weather.

America has famous cities, like New York, which is home to well-known art museums and monuments, like the Statue of Liberty.

Los Angeles in America is known for movies and famous actors who live in a neighborhood called Hollywood.

Lots of US cities have yellow taxis.

This is a clapper board, used to mark moments when directing a movie.

HOLLYWOOD

Statue of Liberty

Add the torch on top of the hand.

Imagine the statue as a person with a blob body. It's standing on a rectangular platform.

Continue to draw squiggly lines on top of the blob to create the outfit. Use the blob to guide your lines!

Bald eagle

The bald eagle symbolizes strength and freedom in the United States of America.

The base of the bald eagle is a jelly-bean shape with a small circular head.

Draw two more jelly beans for the wings. Add triangles for the neck feathers, beak, and feet.

For the last part, draw in long rectangular shapes for the feathers on the wings and a shorter version for the tail.

Cities in the American Northwest are close to mountains and forests, so the weather is cold and rainy.

Seattle is one of the well-known cities in the Northwest. There's a famous tower called the Space Needle, which looks a bit like a spaceship!

Orca whale

Orca whales are large dolphins found along the West Coast of North America. They are much bigger than dolphins and have a unique black-and-white pattern.

Draw an orca whale by starting with a circle. Then add the curved body.

Draw wavy lines to make a pattern on the orca whale. Use one dark and one light color to fill in your drawing.

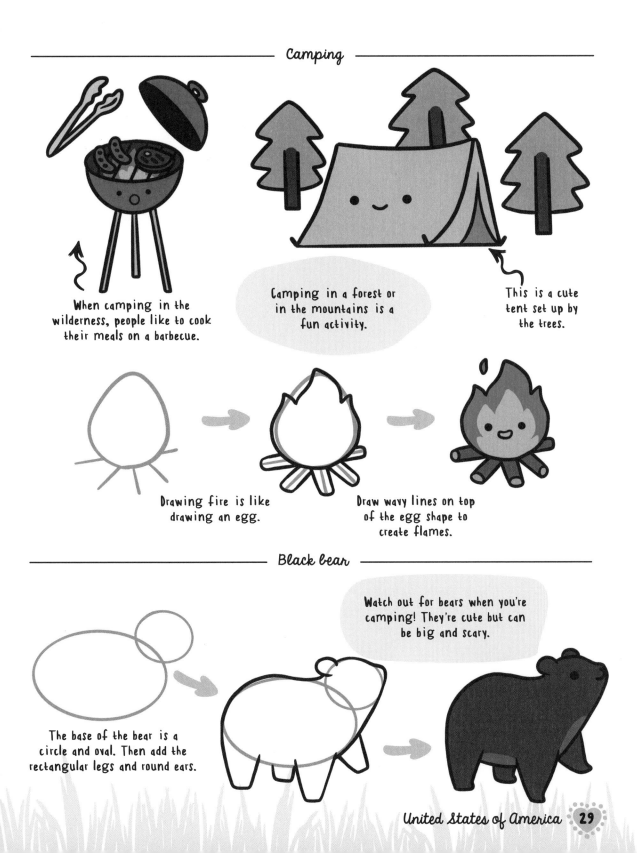

Camping

When camping in the wilderness, people like to cook their meals on a barbecue.

Camping in a forest or in the mountains is a fun activity.

This is a cute tent set up by the trees.

Drawing fire is like drawing an egg.

Draw wavy lines on top of the egg shape to create flames.

Black bear

Watch out for bears when you're camping! They're cute but can be big and scary.

The base of the bear is a circle and oval. Then add the rectangular legs and round ears.

America has the most amusement parks in the world. Amusement parks have games, rides, and yummy food!

Cheesy pepperoni pizza

Fluffy cotton candy

Hamburger with lettuce, tomato, cheese, and a patty.

The Ferris wheel

Add smaller circles and more lines.

A Ferris wheel is a ride at an amusement park. Start with a circle and an "X."

Add little cabins where the lines intersect. People sit inside the cabins!

Canyons and cacti

There are hot canyons and red rocks in the American Southwest.

You can draw cactus plants in several ways. This cactus is upright with two arms.

Add little prickly lines when you've completed the shape.

Some cacti are smaller, fatter, and have flowers.

Longhorn

Longhorns were the first cows in America. The longhorn is known for its long, wide horns.

 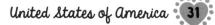

Hawaii is an American island in the Pacific Ocean. It's the only tropical American state with humid weather, special fruits, and rain forests. There are also lots of volcanoes in Hawaii.

The Hawaiian hibiscus flower is, not surprisingly, native to Hawaii!

Hula dancing

The Hawaiian hibiscus is a popular flower.

Draw the base of a person. The head is a circle and the body is like a gumdrop.

Draw repeated lines around the bottom half of the body for the dancer's grass skirt. Don't forget to add a little crop top.

Finish your beautiful hula outfit with flower garlands around the neck and ankle, then add a flower to your dancer's hair.

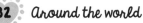

Volcano

Start with a rectangle, then add curved lines going downward.

Draw oozing lava on top of the rectangular base.

Finish off with a cute face and a puff of hot air.

Tropical treats

A rambutan has a spiky-looking shell, but inside it's sweet!

Because of the tropical weather, Hawaii can grow tasty, exotic fruit. Here are some of my colorful favorites!

Mangoes are juicy and sweet. Great for dessert with some ice cream.

Hawaii has warm waters with large waves, perfect for surfers and swimmers.

Let's ride big waves!

Lots of pineapples are grown in Hawaii!

MEXICO

Mexico is a colorful country between North and South America. People love visiting Mexico for the vibrant food, outfits, and ancient buildings left behind by the Mayan and Aztec peoples. The country is also famous for its Day of the Dead celebrations.

The Mexican flag

Cute taco shell filled with ground beef.

People in Mexico like to eat tortillas and taco shells filled with ground beef or chicken, salsa, cilantro, cheese, and a squirt of lime.

Chihuahuas are small dogs from Mexico.

Day of the Dead outfits are very colorful.

A sombrero protects against the hot sun.

The Aztecs built temples at the top of tall pyramids where they could worship their gods.

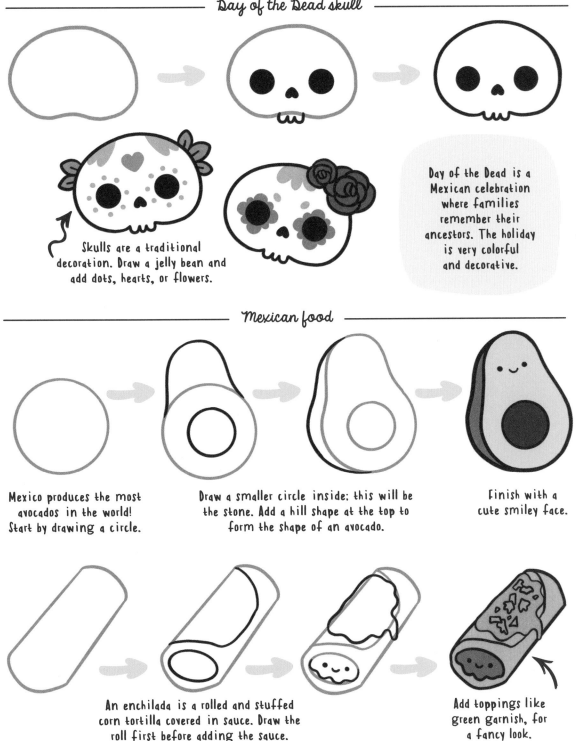

Skulls are a traditional
decoration. Draw a jelly bean and
add dots, hearts, or flowers.

Day of the Dead is a
Mexican celebration
where families
remember their
ancestors. The holiday
is very colorful
and decorative.

Mexican food

Mexico produces the most
avocados in the world!
Start by drawing a circle.

Draw a smaller circle inside; this will be
the stone. Add a hill shape at the top to
form the shape of an avocado.

Finish with a
cute smiley face.

An enchilada is a rolled and stuffed
corn tortilla covered in sauce. Draw the
roll first before adding the sauce.

Add toppings like
green garnish, for
a fancy look.

Draw the base of a person, using a circle and rectangles.

Draw a jelly bean on top of the head; this will be the hat.

Add a peanut shape to start the cello.

Now for the tricky parts: the details! Add these to the outfit and the cello one at a time.

Continue drawing details, like the pattern of the hat and the colors on the face. Draw in the strings of the cello.

The base of the Aztec bird is made up of round shapes. Start with the head and add the body, wings, and legs.

Draw a large headpiece on top of the head. Add in feathers around the head, wings, body, and tail.

The bird warrior was a part of the Aztec culture. It symbolized strength, bravery, and competitiveness.

Add jewelry and feather details.

Aztec clothing uses bright colors, especially green!

BRAZIL

Brazil is the biggest country in South America. There you will find the world's largest rain forest, called the Amazon, home to many colorful animals like tree frogs, sloths, and toucans.

The Brazilian flag

Christ the Redeemer is a giant statue in Rio de Janeiro.

Sloths may be slow, but they are very cute.

What an amazing carnival costume!

Did you know that Brazil is one of the largest countries in the world, by population and by size?

Toucans live in the Amazon. They have large, bright beaks!

The world's biggest carnival takes place every year in Rio de Janeiro. People wear colorful costumes, play music, and dance in the street. It's like a big birthday party!

Exotic plants live in the Amazon, like this Heliconia (known as the lobster plant).

Tree frog

Let's draw a colorful tree frog! Start with an egg-shaped body and add two small circles for the eyes.

Connect the eyes with the body using one line. Add the limbs.

Complete your frog by drawing patterns on its back and letting it sit on a giant lily pad.

The lily pad is a circle with a triangle cut out of it.

Flying monkey

Start your flying monkey with two ovals. This will be the head and face.

Add a circle body and a blob tail.

Draw on the fluffy hair and add details to the face.

The flying monkey has a peach color face that stands out amongst its darker hair!

Jaguar

Begin by drawing a circle for the head, with an oval snout.

The body is like a jelly bean. Add the limbs, tail, and face.

For the spots, draw circles, dots, and moon shapes.

Crocodile

I like drawing crocodiles because they're shaped like bananas.

Add little triangles to create scales on the back of the crocodile.

Did you know that the difference between crocs and alligators is that crocs show their teeth?

You can add more scales to the body using a darker shade of green.

Feijoada stew

Feijoada is a stew of beans with pork sausages. On the table are other small dishes!

A large pot for the stew

Orange slices

Garlic

Vegetables

Rice

Christ the Redeemer

Christ the Redeemer is a large statue of Jesus made by the sculptor Paul Landowski. Look at how small the people are compared to the statue!

Draw the base of a person standing on rectangles. The arms are triangles.

On top of the base, draw wavy lines that make up the outfit. Keep adding lines to show the creases of the clothing.

Little people

PERU

Peru is in South America, like Brazil and Chile. Nearly half of the country is covered by the Amazon rain forest, so you can bet there are cute animals. Peru is famous for its llamas and alpacas that roam around the ancient city of Machu Picchu.

The Peruvian flag

Machu Picchu is a famous ancient city that was built by the Incas. It is high up in the Andes mountains of Peru.

Peruvian fried donut with some sweet jelly.

People in Peru like to use colorful saddlebags on their llamas. They also put garlands around their necks and hang tassels from their ears.

People sometimes wear special clothes in Peru. This is their national costume. The women wear colorful capes, shawls, skirts, and hats. This girl is wearing a special cape called a manta, and a montera, which is a hat that you tie under your chin.

Draw a circle head with an oval body.

Next add the limbs and face.

The Andean bear has a unique pattern on its face that also runs down its chest.

Color most of the fur dark gray, then add the small pattern on the face and chest in light tan.

Begin by making a circle head and a large oval body.

Connect the head and body using curved lines. Add the flippers and tail.

Off the coast of Peru there are thousands of sea lions! You can even go swimming with them.

Guinea pigs

Guinea pigs come from the grasslands and lower slopes of the Andes Mountains in Peru and other countries in South America. They are cute, fluffy, and make great pets. Did you know they can make lots of sounds such as wheeking and purring?

The base of the alpaca is made up of many circles and ovals.

On top of the base, draw in lumps of fur. They look like clouds!

Alpacas have soft, fluffy wool, which people use to make warm clothes. You can color the accessories any way you prefer: I chose red, green, and yellow!

Draw in accessories like a necklace and a saddlebag.

Add decorations on the ears.

Color in the accessories with bright colors!

CHILE

Chile is the world's longest country, with the Andes Mountains on one side and the Pacific Ocean on the other. It's also home to a 600-mile desert, the Atacama, which is the driest desert on Earth.

The Chilean flag

Be as cool as a cucumber.

The Mano del Desierto is a giant sculpture of a hand located in the Atacama Desert in Chile. It was made by the artist Mario Irarrázabal. Look at how big it is compared to those small people!

You'll be surprised to know that desert people like to grow tomatoes and cucumbers.

Cowboys in Chile are called huasos. They wear special straw hats and enjoy riding at rodeos.

Stargazing is a popular activity in Chile because the deserts have clear and open skies. The largest telescopes (bigger than the Statue of Liberty) are in Chile!

There are four telescopes called The Very Large Telescopes. They look like these boxes.

Draw a planet!

To draw a small telescope, make a cylinder.

Add the telescope stand by creating a triangle at the bottom.

Draw more lines for the stand and start erasing the extra lines.

The first step is to draw the horse. Make a jelly-bean body and add the limbs.

Add more limbs and hair to the tail.

Once you have the base of the horse, draw a person riding. The body is like a gumdrop.

Add the details of the person's clothing and the horse's saddle.

Chilean rodeo is a sport where two horse riders race around an arena to catch a calf.

 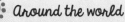

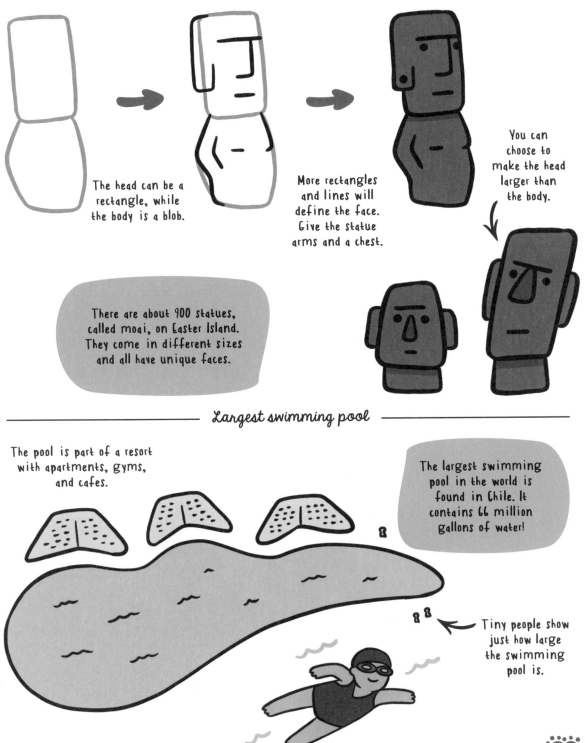

The head can be a rectangle, while the body is a blob.

More rectangles and lines will define the face. Give the statue arms and a chest.

You can choose to make the head larger than the body.

There are about 900 statues, called moai, on Easter Island. They come in different sizes and all have unique faces.

Largest swimming pool

The pool is part of a resort with apartments, gyms, and cafes.

The largest swimming pool in the world is found in Chile. It contains 66 million gallons of water!

Tiny people show just how large the swimming pool is.

SOUTH AFRICA

South Africa is home to giant and fierce animals, like the African buffalo, elephants, with their huge ears, exotic birds, and Cape penguins—South Africa is like a giant zoo!

The South African flag

South African yellow rice in a cute bowl.

South African mask

A cute baby rhinoceros.

Johannesburg in South Africa has lots of colorful houses.

Sawubona is a greeting that means "I see you!"

This man belongs to the Ndebele people of South Africa, and is wearing the traditional costume.

An African elephant

Lion

Make the base of the lion a cat with floppy ears.

Add the fluffy mane. Imagine making a cloud around the lion's head.

Lions are large cats that like taking naps in grasslands. The male lions have manes. To draw a female lion, draw a big cat without a mane.

Even the tail is fluffy!

African buffalo

Like the lion, the African buffalo has a similar base. Instead, draw different ears.

Draw in long wide horns and the details on the hooves.

Color the horns a lighter brown to make them stand out from the body.

Start drawing a penguin by making a circle head and oval body.

Add flippers and a beak.

You can play around with the patterns on the penguin! Make it wavy or dotted.

Cape penguins only live in Southern Africa. They hang out on the beach and eat squid.

——— Traditional and modern dress ———

The Zulu is the largest tribe in South Africa. Traditional Zulu dress for men includes animal skins and feathers. Men wear different skins depending on their status in the tribe.

South-African fashion mixes modern design and traditional crafts.

This bag uses traditional materials like grass.

African styles include bold colors and shapes.

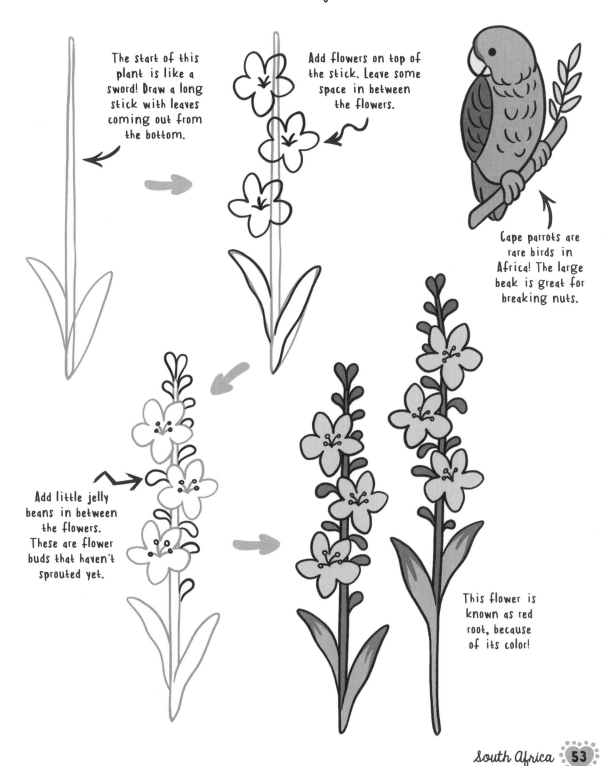

The start of this plant is like a sword! Draw a long stick with leaves coming out from the bottom.

Add flowers on top of the stick. Leave some space in between the flowers.

Cape parrots are rare birds in Africa! The large beak is great for breaking nuts.

Add little jelly beans in between the flowers. These are flower buds that haven't sprouted yet.

This flower is known as red root, because of its color!

Soccer

When players hit the ball into a goal, they say "Laduma!"

Draw the base of a person. This person looks like they're running!

Add squares for the clothing. Draw in a competitive face!

Draw a soccer ball using hexagon shapes.

South African masks

Starting a mask is easy: just make an oval.

Draw in details like the face and symbols. Colors will also make your mask special.

Masks can symbolize families, animals, or spirits. They can represent events too.

Bunny Chow is bread filled with curry! Start by drawing the hollowed-out bread.

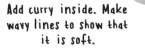

Add curry inside. Make wavy lines to show that it is soft.

Add a green garnish on top.

The curry is a warm color, while the bread is brown.

Bobotie is a dish of baked meat with an eggy topping.

A braai is a South African barbecue. It's an outdoor social event where people gather around a fire for an entire evening. The smoke adds to the flavor of the food.

Draw shapes like circles, triangles, and rectangles. There's meat and vegetables at a braai.

ETHIOPIA

Ethiopia is a country in East Africa, and is believed to be the birthplace of coffee. This region of Africa has the largest population of livestock in the whole continent, and Ethiopia is home to goats, sheep, pigs, and camels.

The Ethiopian flag

Coffee beans are crushed to make coffee drinks.

In the National Museum in Addis Ababa there's a skeleton called Lucy, which is over three million years old.

This is St. George's Church, which is one of 11 churches that were carved out of rock in Lalibela, in Ethiopia, hundreds of years ago.

Traditionally, people wear long clothing or tunics to cover their bodies. This is part of their religion, and also protects them from the heat.

The habesha kemis is a traditional dress in Ethiopia. It has beautiful patterns.

Draw three overlapping circles. These are the breads that will hold the toppings.

Draw the toppings on top of the bread. You can draw blobs or small circles.

Injera is flatbread that is traditionally eaten with sides like stew, curry, and vegetables. The sides are put on top of the bread.

EGYPT

Egypt is in North Africa. It has hot deserts and busy cities, like Cairo, with bustling markets. Egypt is famous for many ancient monuments such as temples, pyramids, and a giant statue called the Sphinx. The famous River Nile runs through Egypt—without this huge river, all of Egypt would be a desert.

The Great Pyramid of Giza is Egypt's largest pyramid. It was built for the Pharaoh Khufu.

I'm more than 4,000 years old.

The Sphinx is a huge statue near the Great Pyramid at Giza.

Pharaohs and other important people in ancient Egypt were buried in a special coffin called a sarcophagus.

Most families had a pet cat in ancient Egypt, because they thought it would bring good luck.

A traditional Egyptian boat is called a felucca.

The Sphinx

The head of the Sphinx is a circle and the body is a rounded rectangle.

Draw a semicircle around the head and give the Sphinx arms.

Finish with a rectangle and an ear on the head.

The Sphinx is a mythical creature with the head of a human and the body of a lion.

Pharaoh coffin

Start by drawing the head of the coffin.

Add more shapes around the head.

Once you have the head, draw the body—it's like a curved triangle.

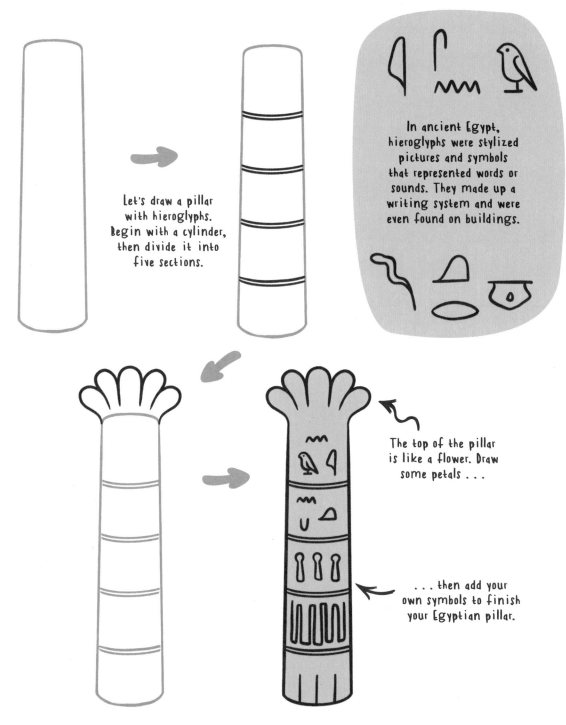

Let's draw a pillar with hieroglyphs. Begin with a cylinder, then divide it into five sections.

In ancient Egypt, hieroglyphs were stylized pictures and symbols that represented words or sounds. They made up a writing system and were even found on buildings.

The top of the pillar is like a flower. Draw some petals . . .

. . . then add your own symbols to finish your Egyptian pillar.

Cotton

Egyptian cotton is handpicked and super soft. Cotton is used to make clothing and in stuffed animals.

This is the stem of a cotton plant.

This cute teddy bear is stuffed with cotton.

Draw three circles with stems coming out of the bottom.

Draw clouds around the circles to form the cotton. These are called cotton bolls.

Give them all cute faces!

Ful medames

Ful medames is a type of stew cooked with beans and spices.

To draw this dish, start with the bowl and then add the beans.

Add your favorite vegetables, like peppers or onions, to top it off.

Kushari is an Egyptian dish with macaroni, tomato sauce, and rice!

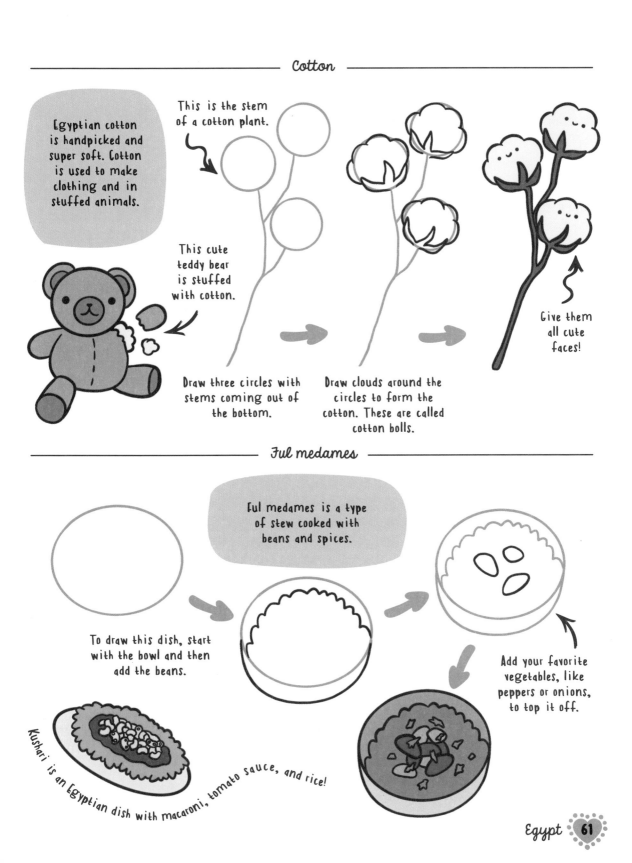

MOROCCO

Like Ethiopia and Egypt, Morocco is in Africa. It is a very hot, dry, and dusty country, with lots of deserts. The Berber people have lived in Morocco for centuries. People in Morocco like to drink a special mint tea sweetened with sugar.

The Moroccan flag

You'll find all sorts of animals in the desert, like wild monkeys, boars, snakes, chameleons, and camels.

The sand dunes in Morocco's Sahara Desert are very tall.

SALAM ALAIKUM means "Peace upon you!"

To protect themselves from the sun, people in Morocco cover their heads with hats and scarves.

Camels are still sometimes used to carry people and goods across the desert.

Camel

To draw a camel, begin with a round body and rectangular limbs.

Don't forget the oval head.

Add two hills on the back. These are the camel's humps.

You can draw the saddle on top too.

Draw the details of the saddle and add a bridle with long reins.

Continue adding details like patterns and tassels to make the saddle and bridle look fancy.

Desert clothes

Loose clothing is multipurpose: it can cover your entire body but still be light! It also protects you from the sun and lets the wind breeze through.

Fancy teapot

Let's take the teapot step by step. Draw a fat oval with a skinny oval on top.

Add a triangular hat for the teapot lid, then draw the curved handle and spout.

The last stage of the teapot is drawing wavy lines on the body. You can get fancy by drawing a plate with mint leaves and a glass to drink the tea from!

Moroccan food

You can store spices in a terracotta pot.

A kaaba is an almond cookie.

A chebakia is a sesame cookie shaped like a flower.

A tagine is a heavy cooking pot.

Snake charmer

Snake charmers in Morocco play an instrument called a pungi to hypnotize snakes (usually cobras).

Fennec fox

The color of the fennec fox's fur helps it blend into the sand in the desert where it lives.

You know the drill: draw a circle and an oval!

The ears and tail are similar triangle shapes.

Add the long limbs and fuzzy fur around the fox.

Color your fox a light tan.

Morocco 65

SPAIN

Spain is in Europe and has the huge Atlantic Ocean on one side and the Mediterranean Sea on the other. The capital of Spain is a famous city called Madrid. Spain is a colorful and exciting country where people enjoy music, dancing, and eating food like paella and tapas.

The Spanish flag

Paella Valenciana is a Spanish rice dish. You can find vegetables, clams, and seafood in it.

Bullfighters use a big, colorful cape to make the bull angry and charge at them!

Flamenco is a Spanish dance that is performed to guitar music. It is very exciting and energetic.

A flamenco guitar is made from Spanish wood.

A flamenco dancer wears a long, frilly skirt and special shoes that make a loud sound when they touch the floor.

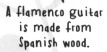

Start by drawing the upper part of the dancer. The body is a curved rectangle and the head is a circle. The arms are just lines for now.

Next, connect the lines to form arms. Draw a large jelly bean for the dress.

Add waves for the frills of the dress.

Repeat the wavy lines to create a massive, frilly skirt.

Fans

Spanish fans are bright and colorful, and often decorated with lace. The fans are used in flamenco dancing.

ITALY

Italy is rich in culture, food, and art. Some of the most ancient and beautiful architecture can be found in the capital city of Rome. Italy has the most historical sites compared to other countries in the world.

The Italian flag

This is a statue of a cherub, which is a baby angel.

Italians love food and Italy is famous for pizza, pasta, and ice cream (which they call gelato).

Pasta dishes are popular in Italy. This one has cute red tomatoes!

You can put any kind of topping on your pizza, like meat, vegetables, or cheese.

What's your favorite topping?

Columns are upright pillars that hold buildings up. They are iconic in Roman architecture.

Ciao is a greeting!

Add lines behind the scooter to show that it's speeding along. Vroom vroom!

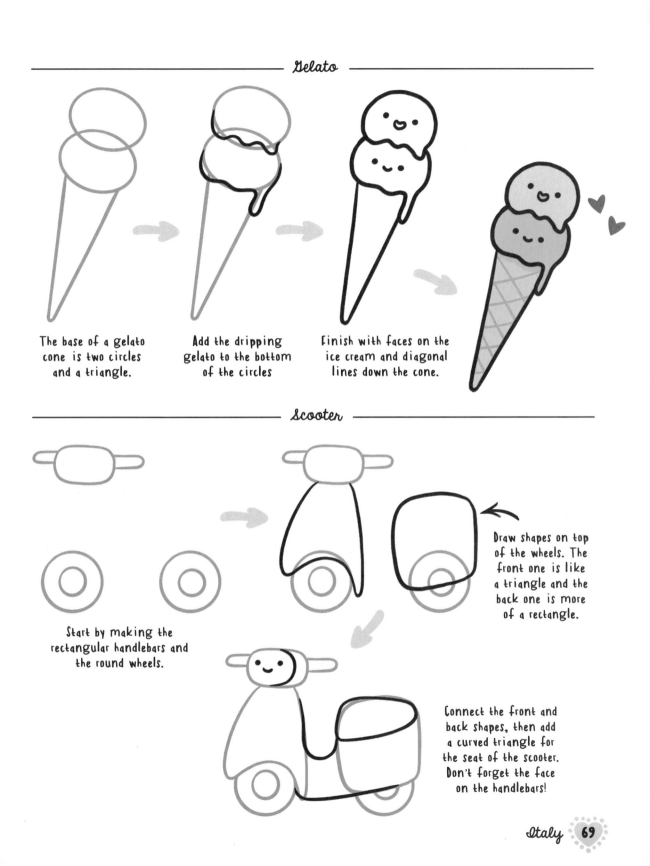

The base of a gelato
cone is two circles
and a triangle.

Add the dripping
gelato to the bottom
of the circles

Finish with faces on the
ice cream and diagonal
lines down the cone.

— *Scooter* —

Start by making the
rectangular handlebars and
the round wheels.

Draw shapes on top
of the wheels. The
front one is like
a triangle and the
back one is more
of a rectangle.

Connect the front and
back shapes, then add
a curved triangle for
the seat of the scooter.
Don't forget the face
on the handlebars!

FRANCE

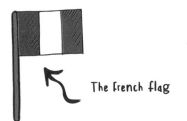

The French flag

France is known for its art, fashion, and buildings. The capital city is Paris, also called the City of Love because of its romantic vibes. A lot of France is covered with forests and farms too!

Macarons are just one of the little cakes you can buy from a French patisserie.

The Eiffel Tower in Paris was opened in 1889.

There are amazing pastries in France, including croissants, little cakes, and crepes (both sweet and savory). In addition, French people also like garlicky snails called escargots!

Hot-air balloons were invented in France by the Montgolfier brothers in the late 1780s.

A baguette is a thin stick of French bread.

France is very famous for its talented artists.

French people like to eat croissants for breakfast. Yum!

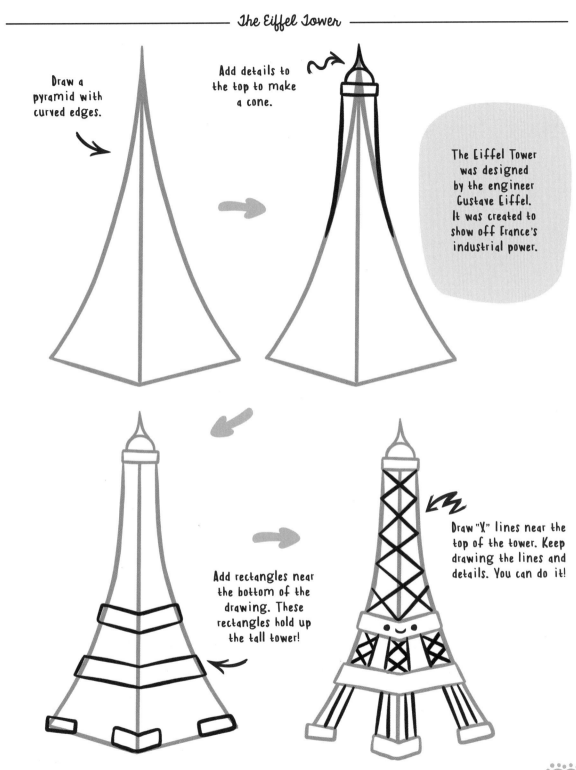

Draw a pyramid with curved edges.

Add details to the top to make a cone.

The Eiffel Tower was designed by the engineer Gustave Eiffel. It was created to show off France's industrial power.

Add rectangles near the bottom of the drawing. These rectangles hold up the tall tower!

Draw "X" lines near the top of the tower. Keep drawing the lines and details. You can do it!

Another name for a French Bulldog is a Frenchie!

Add a cute face and tongue sticking out.

Draw a circle head and oval body. Add rectangular legs and triangular ears and tail. The muzzle is a bendy jelly bean.

Color the ears and tongue with a light pink.

Chartreux cat

This is a very chubby cat. Draw a large oval body and a small circle for the head.

The Chartreux is a rare breed of cat from France.

Draw triangular ears on top of the head. Make cute chubby cheeks by adding ovals to the face.

Draw the cat's limbs to one side to show that it is laying down.

Paris is a very fashionable city, and is home to many famous clothes designers.

Checkers

Coats

Ankle boots

Beret hat

Feathers

French Revolution time

Frilly dress

NETHERLANDS

The Netherlands is a small country in Europe, which is very close to France and Germany. The Netherlands is famous for its windmills, Edam cheese, tulips, and wooden clogs.

The Dutch flag

The Dutch love to grow colorful tulips.

Wooden windmills have been used to pump water from wetlands in the Netherlands for 600 years.

Wooden clogs are part of the national costume of the Netherlands.

The Dutch traditional costume includes simple pinafores, trousers, and pointed hats.

The Netherlands is a very flat country, which is probably why people like to ride bikes everywhere!

Edam cheese comes in big rounded cylinders.

 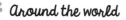

Dutch lady

Draw the base of a person with their arms outward.

On top of the base, draw a triangular hat. Add the details of the clothing too.

Continue drawing in details, such as the sides of the hat, the face, and the body.

Windmill

Begin the windmill by drawing a gumdrop.

Create a rectangle below the gumdrop. For the blades, draw an "X." Add a little rectangle for the door.

Draw rectangles at the ends of the "X" and finish with a cute face.

UNITED KINGDOM

The United Kingdom is made up of four countries: England, Scotland, Wales, and Northern Ireland. It is an island off the coast of Europe and is famous for its history, countryside, castles, old buildings, and literature. The capital city of England is London, which is where the Queen lives in a palace called Buckingham Palace.

The Union flag

If you visit London, you will see lots of red buses taking people around the city.

The different parts of the UK are famous for different things. For example, Wales has the Welsh Dragon as an emblem, while Scotland is famous for its plaid and bagpipe music.

The Tower of London is a very old castle and prison in London.

Doesn't this look tasty?

♥ yum!

Nessie, a monster that looks like a dinosaur, is said to live in the waters of Loch Ness, in Scotland.

Fish and chips is a hot dish made of fried fish and fries.

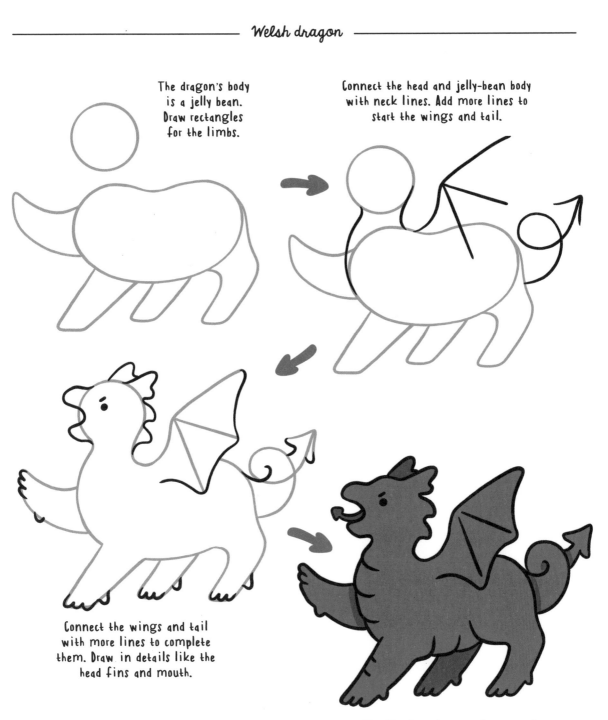

The dragon's body is a jelly bean. Draw rectangles for the limbs.

Connect the head and jelly-bean body with neck lines. Add more lines to start the wings and tail.

Connect the wings and tail with more lines to complete them. Draw in details like the head fins and mouth.

The final touches are the stomach and front leg lines and the triangular tongue.

United Kingdom · 77

Cream tea

Draw an oval.

Add the jam. It's like drawing a cloud.

Draw a larger cloud on top. This will be the cream.

Afternoon tea is a popular tradition in the UK. People like to eat little sandwiches, biscuits with cream and jam, and delicious cakes, all with a cup of tea.

Puffin

Finish off with lines on the body for the patterns of the feathers.

The base of the puffin is a circle for the head, an oval for the body, and a triangle for the beak.

Continue adding details like the triangle feet and tail.

Puffins nest in rocks by the sea, and dive into the water to catch fish for their dinner.

The details of the outfit are very important. Notice all the small rectangles and crosses I am adding to the drawing.

Create the base of your person by drawing a circle and rectangles.

Draw a gumdrop hat and start adding more limb details.

Finally, give your person a bagpipe to play! Color the clothing with a fun plaid pattern.

Plaid pattern

To draw a plaid pattern, start with a base color, like red.

Add horizontal and vertical lines using a darker color. Space the lines out evenly.

The last step is to add a thin line in between the darker lines. Pick a brighter color for these lines!

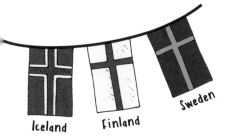

Iceland   Finland   Sweden

Denmark   Norway   Faroe Islands

NORDICS

The Nordics are made up of many different countries, including Finland, Sweden, Norway, Denmark, Iceland, and the Faroe Islands. They each have their own flag and capital city. Some of these countries are in the Arctic Circle, which means it gets very cold.

Caribou have very big antlers.

It snows a lot in Nordic countries, and people enjoy skidding along in a sleigh drawn by caribou. These are sometimes called reindeer.

Vikings were pirates from the late 8th century. They had ships with large sails.

The Vikings carved animal heads into the bows of their ships.

A Viking armed with a round shield and a long ax. This Viking warrior is wearing a horned helmet.

A troll is a creature from Nordic folklore that lives in mountains and caves.

Every troll begins with a simple shape. The tree troll starts with a gumdrop.

Draw jagged shapes around the gumdrop. Imagine these are messy leaves.

Continue drawing shapes around the troll to add more leaves and put two triangular trees on top of its head.

Add more jagged lines to turn the triangles into trees.

The rock troll has a hexagonal shape.

The mountain troll has a triangular shape.

The start of a flower crown is a donut shape!

Add large and small flowers to the donut.

Draw leaves and bumpy lines for the greenery that covers the crown.

Flower crown

People build tall maypoles and decorate them with leaves and flowers for Sweden's Midsummer Festival. They dress in traditional costume and wear beautiful flower crowns.

People dance around the maypole.

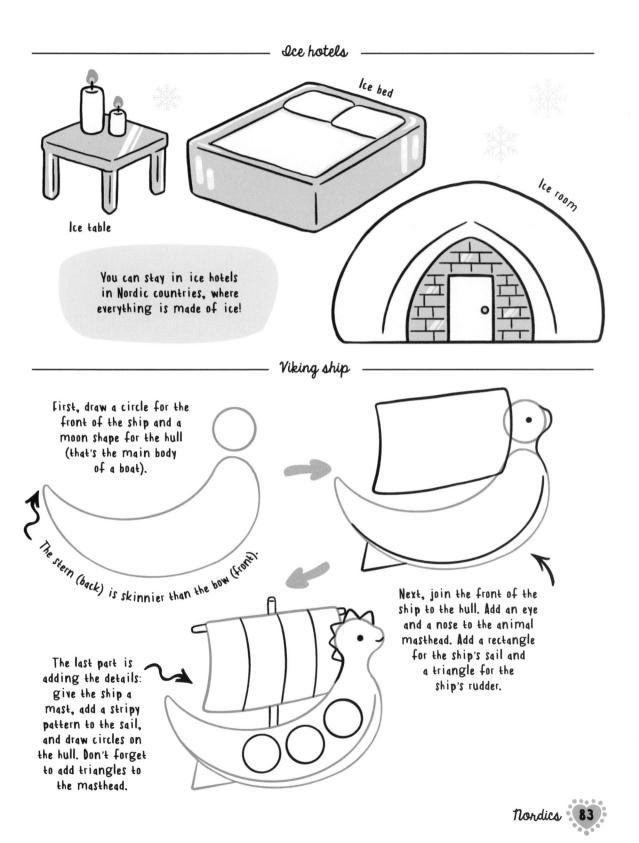

Ice hotels

Ice table

Ice bed

Ice room

You can stay in ice hotels in Nordic countries, where everything is made of ice!

Viking ship

First, draw a circle for the front of the ship and a moon shape for the hull (that's the main body of a boat).

The stern (back) is skinnier than the bow (front).

Next, join the front of the ship to the hull. Add an eye and a nose to the animal masthead. Add a rectangle for the ship's sail and a triangle for the ship's rudder.

The last part is adding the details: give the ship a mast, add a stripy pattern to the sail, and draw circles on the hull. Don't forget to add triangles to the masthead.

HUNGARY

Hungary is in the middle of Europe. It is completely landlocked, which means that it has no seas around it. The capital of Hungary is Budapest and the River Danube, which is over 1,770 miles long, runs straight through the city.

The Hungarian flag

Hungary has high-quality meat foods, like chicken. Of course, it also has pork, beef, and others.

Chicken Paprikash is a dish of chicken in a creamy paprika sauce.

The Budapest Chain Bridge is guarded by two huge stone lions at each end.

This colorful puzzle was invented by Ernő Rubik, who is Hungarian.

The largest lake in Hungary is called Lake Balaton. It is popular with people who enjoy watersports.

Water polo is a popular sport in Hungary.

Draw a slanted
square.

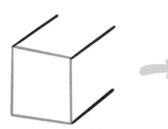

Draw three diagonal lines
coming out from the corners.
Make sure these lines are all
the same length.

Close off the cube
by connecting the
diagonal lines.

Draw two connected lines
on the top and on the
side of the cube.

Draw another two lines on
the top and front.

Add two lines to the front
and side of the cube, and
a smiley face.

Hungarian trifle

Lots of Hungarians love
ice cream and Somlói
Galuska, a trifle dessert.

Somlói Galuska

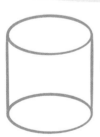

Start this dessert
drawing with
a cylinder.

Add a blob of
pastry cream
inside the
cylinder.

Next, draw some
zigzags! These
will be the
chocolate drizzle.

Lastly, add some cake
crumbs in the shape
of cubes.

RUSSIA

Russia is the biggest country in the world, and is part of both the European continent and the Asian continent. Russia's capital city Moscow has some amazing landmarks, including the Kremlin fortress, Red Square, and St. Basil's Cathedral.

The Russian flag

There are lots of brown bears roaming wild in Russia.

St. Basil's Cathedral is very colorful, like other special buildings in Moscow.

Babushka dolls in the same set are always decorated with the same colors and pattern. Russian emperors had jeweled eggs made as Easter gifts for their wives and mothers.

Babushka dolls get smaller and smaller and smaller, placed one inside the other.

Fabergé egg

Russian dancing

The Russian Cossack dance is very energetic, and you have to be fit to do it. People dress up in traditional costumes for folk dances like this.

Babushka doll

The babushka doll is made of two circles. The bottom circle is slightly larger.

Connect the two circles together. Add a third circle for the face, plus two eyes and a mouth.

Now for the patterns. Add little ovals to start drawing flowers.

Add lines around the ovals . . .

. . . and finish with some leaves.

Balalaika

Instruments such as the balalaika and the accordion are played in Russian folk music.

Accordion

Balalaika player

Begin by drawing the base of a person.

Add a large triangle on top of your person; this is where the balalaika will be.

Bring the player to life with a face and arm, and add the neck to the balalaika.

Finish with the details of your player's hair and clothes, and add the strings and tuning keys to the instrument.

Amur leopard

Russia is home to some very big cats, including the Amur tiger and the Amur leopard.

Draw a circle for the head, triangles for the ears, and an oval for the body.

Add the front and back legs. Imagine them as rounded rectangles, with an extra oval connecting the back leg to the body.

Now that you have your tiger, add the stripes! The stripes make a pretty pattern when they are spaced evenly over the body.

Amur tiger

The final pattern on the tiger is the light color around its mouth and down its chest.

SOUTH KOREA

South Korea is a country in East Asia and the capital city is called Seoul. It is almost completely surrounded by ocean. Most of the country is covered with hills and mountains—the highest mountain is called Hallasan. There are also amazing mountains in the Seoraksan National Park, where you can visit the Great Unification Buddha.

The Korean flag

The royal house in South Korea is called Gyeongbok Palace. It is in Seoul, the capital city.

Kimbap is a popular Korean picnic food, made from cooked rice and other ingredients wrapped in dried seaweed.

The traditional dress of South Korea is called hanbok. The costumes for both men and women are very colorful.

Korean beauty products are popular around the world.

Hanbok

First, draw the base of your person and the gumdrop-shaped dress.

Next, draw two rectangular arms and add some hair—this lady has her hair in a bun.

Finally, add the details to the dress, including an apron and a large bow.

Beauty products

Let's draw a small lip gloss container by starting with a cylinder.

Add the cap line and some cat ears.

Finish with a face and sparkles!

Drawing lipstick can be cute when you add a panda face!

Open the cap to reveal the lipstick!

Begin with an oval.

Add panda ears . . .

. . . and a face, and hands.

Korean pop, or K-pop, is fun music performed by young and talented artists. It is popular with young people.

When drawing a K-pop band, think of cool poses for your group!

Draw the base of your people . . .

. . . then add fun clothing. Group clothing doesn't have to match.

Add musical notes around your band.

Sometimes Korean bands will make stuffed animals that are based on them. This cat has the same colors as one of the band member's hair!

At concerts, fans will bring signs and glow sticks to wave!

Korean barbecues are lots of fun because the meat and vegetables are grilled in the center of the table and everyone can join in and share.

Kimchi is very popular in Korea. It is made from salted and fermented vegetables such as cabbage and Korean radish, with lots of seasonings like garlic and ginger.

Start your kimchi with two rectangles.

Add squiggly lines around the rectangles and add faces.

Color in the kimchi with different shades of red and orange.

JAPAN

Japan is made up of a chain of islands along the eastern coast of Asia. The capital city Tokyo is found on the biggest island, and known for its bustling vibe. You can also visit other cities such as Kyoto, where you will find historical sights and temples. You can travel on the super-fast bullet train, the Shinkansen.

The Japanese flag

Cherry blossom

There are over 100 active volcanoes in Japan, including the famous, snow-capped, Mount Fuji.

Mount Fuji

Kimono

Maneki-neko, the lucky cat

A Japanese rice ball wrapped in nori (edible seaweed) is called onigiri.

Ramen is a Japanese noodle soup.

Japanese shrine

Nigiri is a type of sushi, with a piece of tuna fish or salmon placed over the rice.

The Shiba Inu is a Japanese dog breed. People sometimes put a colorful scarf around its neck.

The base of the Shiba Inu is ovals and triangles.

Next, draw on a triangular scarf and round limbs. Don't forget to add a face!

The Shiba Inu breed is known for its cute, curly round tail.

Origami

Start with a rectangle.

The paper crane is made up of many triangles and rectangles.

Begin with a circle and gumdrop. This will be the body and head of your samurai.

Samurai were Japanese warriors in the 12th century. They wore armor and carried a samurai sword, which is special because it is curved and hand carved.

Add the arms and legs . . .

. . . then start the helmet and sword.

Imagine the armor as a group of rectangles. Add them on top of the body.

Finish off with stripe patterns on the armor.

Bonsai is the art of growing miniature trees, which is a very popular hobby in Japan. The most popular trees for bonsai are pine, maple, and blossom trees.

Bonsai trees are known for their interesting trunk shapes. This one looks like a zigzag.

Draw the tree's leaves by adding cloud shapes. Make them different sizes.

Add details, like lines on the trunk and extra cloud shapes.

Cherry and plum trees are often used in bonsai because of their pretty colors.

The final step is to pick a bright color for the leaves!

TAIWAN

Taiwan is a small island country in the Pacific Ocean, east of China. The country has scenic areas, like the Sun Moon Lake, which you can cycle around. Taiwan is also famous for its hot springs and there are about a hundred of these scattered all over the island.

The Taiwanese flag

Taiwanese people really love food, especially bao buns—steamed buns with delicious fillings—and boba cups. Boba was created in Taiwan!

Bao buns are delicious...

...and they always look happy!

Boba cup

This is an iconic building in the capital city Taipei. It's called Taipei 101.

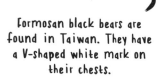

Formosan black bears are found in Taiwan. They have a V-shaped white mark on their chests.

Traditional Taiwanese costumes are very colorful. Both men and women wear long tunics and headdresses.

Market fish sticks

The night market is a fun place to try different kinds of food, like fish sticks. They come in many shapes.

Draw three circles to make this one.

This one has irregular shapes stacked on top of one another.

Boba cups

The base of the boba cup is a gumdrop. Or you can draw a rounded rectangle.

Add circles at the bottom; these are the tapioca pearls.

Make your drink super cute by adding a face!

Boba cups are filled with a special tea and shaken to create a foamy layer on top. Tapioca pearls are added to the tea.

Bao bun

Let's draw a little bao bun. Start with an oval.

Add three bumps on top of the oval. The shape kind of looks like hair!

Add a smiley face and you have a cute little bao bun!

CHINA

China is a vast country in Asia with lots of different climates, including hot tropical regions, very cold zones, and the huge Gobi Desert. In the west of the country, you'll find the Himalayas, which is the world's largest mountain range.

The Chinese flag

The Great Wall of China is over 5,000 miles long and was built to keep invaders out of China.

Paper lantern

Chinese Zodiac

Pagoda

Giant pandas live in the Wolong National Nature Reserve in China.

I always start with a circle for the head. Then connect it to the long body.

Continue expanding the body. Draw the mouth, ears, and front legs.

Add details such as triangular spikes to the dragon's back and tail, and a long horn on its head.

The Chinese dragon is commonly depicted as a snake with four legs. If knowing this helps you to draw your dragon, then just imagine making a snake first!

Make a watermelon shape to start off your dumpling.

Next, draw squiggly lines along the top.

A group food is hot pot, which is a soup that you add ingredients to while you eat. Chinese people will huddle around the pot and add dumplings, meat, fish balls, and vegetables into the hot pot.

I have a most delicious filling.

Vegetables

Dipping sauce

Fish balls

Cabbage and corn

Meat

Mushrooms

Chinese hot pot

Spicy seasoning

Lanterns

Chinese lanterns are made from paper. When the flame at the bottom is lit, the lantern glows and floats away into the night sky.

You can make any lantern with a rounded shape. Choose an oval or a long rectangle.

Once you've chosen your base shape, add rectangles to the top and bottom of the lantern.

Bamboo

Start drawing the bamboo by making a skinny rectangle.

Draw lines sticking out on the sides.

Draw on leaves and add horizontal lines to the stem.

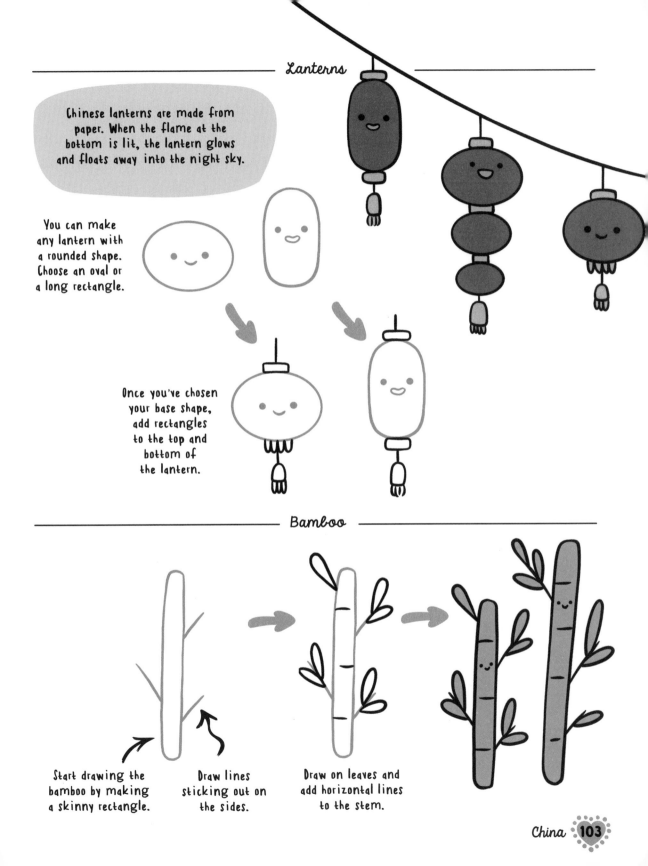

There are 12 signs in the Chinese Zodiac. Your sign depends on the year you were born in. Which sign are you?

All the Zodiac animals have the same base: two ovals stacked on top of each other.

YEAR OF THE MOUSE

FEBRUARY 7, 2008 TO JANUARY 25, 2009 • JANUARY 25, 2020 TO FEBRUARY 11, 2021

YEAR OF THE OX

JANUARY 26, 2009 TO FEBRUARY 13, 2010 • FEBRUARY 12, 2021 TO JANUARY 31, 2022

YEAR OF THE TIGER

FEBRUARY 14, 2010 TO FEBRUARY 2, 2011 • FEBRUARY 1, 2022 TO JANUARY 21, 2023

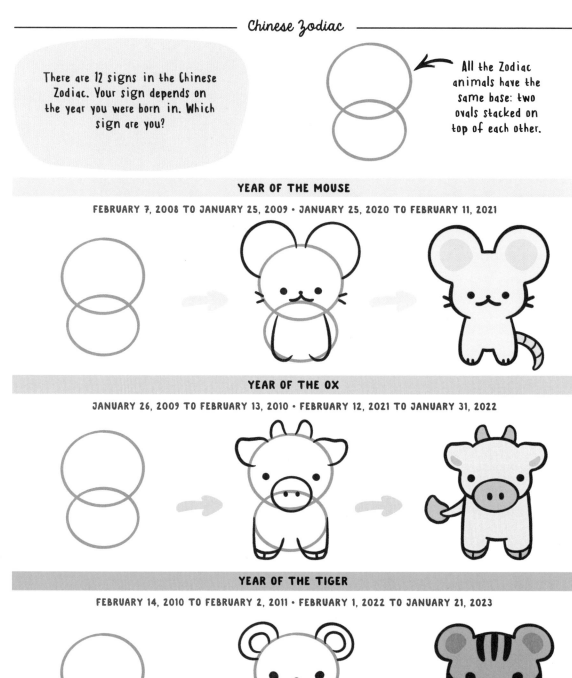

YEAR OF THE RABBIT

FEBRUARY 3, 2011 TO JANUARY 22, 2012 • JANUARY 22, 2023 TO FEBRUARY 9, 2024

YEAR OF THE DRAGON

JANUARY 23, 2012 TO FEBRUARY 9, 2013 • FEBRUARY 10, 2024 TO JANUARY 28, 2025

YEAR OF THE SNAKE

FEBRUARY 10, 2013 TO JANUARY 29, 2014 • JANUARY 29, 2025 TO FEBRUARY 16, 2026

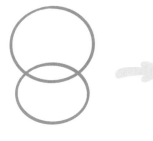

YEAR OF THE HORSE

JANUARY 30, 2014 TO FEBRUARY 18, 2015 • FEBRUARY 17, 2026 TO FEBRUARY 5, 2027

YEAR OF THE SHEEP

FEBRUARY 19, 2015 TO FEBRUARY 7, 2016 • FEBRUARY 6, 2022 TO JANUARY 25, 2028

YEAR OF THE MONKEY

FEBRUARY 8, 2016 TO JANUARY 27, 2017 • JANUARY 26, 2028 TO FEBRUARY 12, 2029

YEAR OF THE CHICKEN

JANUARY 28, 2017 TO FEBRUARY 14, 2018 • FEBRUARY 13, 2029 TO FEBRUARY 2, 2030

YEAR OF THE DOG

FEBRUARY 15, 2018 TO FEBRUARY 4, 2019 • FEBRUARY 3, 2030 TO JANUARY 22, 2031

YEAR OF THE PIG

FEBRUARY 5, 2019 TO JANUARY 24, 2020 • JANUARY 23, 2031 TO FEBRUARY 10, 2032

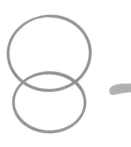

INDIA

The Indian flag

India is a vast country and home to around 1.4 billion people. It is known for being a busy, colorful, religious, and traditional country. There are some famous sites in India, including the Ganges river and the Taj Mahal palace.

Ganesha is the Hindu god of new beginnings and has the head of an elephant. He holds different things, including a bowl of sweets and an ax.

Indian cities are very busy and there is a lot of traffic. Auto rickshaws are used to carry people about. They often only have three wheels.

A lehenga is an Indian outfit made up of a long skirt, a blouse, and a stole (which is a long, wide scarf).

Bollywood is similar to Hollywood in Los Angeles, but the movies are all in Hindi. It is based in Mumbai, India.

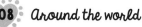

Peacock

The head is a circle and the body is an egg shape.

The tail is like a jelly bean. Make it almost the same size as the body.

The national bird of India is a peacock.

Add the feathers last. When you color them, imagine you are drawing lots of colorful circles.

Yoga

Yoga is a type of exercise where you move your body into different positions. You also have to concentrate on your breathing and staying calm and relaxed.

Indian curry

Curry is an Indian meal made with meat and vegetables, and flavored with hot spices. It is often eaten with rice or a type of bread called naan.

Naan bread

Chicken curry

Rice

Sari dress

Add the final part of the dress over the other arm, then color in the outfit. Add small sparkles, triangles, and dots to make a detailed dress.

Draw the base of a person using a circle and two gumdrops.

Draw on the person's face and their arms. Imagine the arms are rectangles.

Add a sash on top of the dress. This can drape over the shoulder and arm.

First draw a circle and jelly-bean ears.

Next, add on a larger circle for the body and smaller circles for the legs.

Then start drawing on the arms and legs, and add the trunk.

Draw in the details for the hands and hat. The hat is like a gumdrop and triangle.

Add small details, such as jewels on the trunk and hat.

VIETNAM

Vietnam is in Southern Asia. The two largest cities are Ha Noi and Saigon. There are many beautiful landscapes like beaches, deserts, jungles, and bustling cities. The food is also some of the healthiest and tastiest!

The Vietnamese flag

Ha Long Bay is a beautiful ocean bay dotted with tall rock formations. They are like little islands.

Snub-nosed monkey

Ao dai is the traditional outfit of Vietnam.

A Bánh Xèo is a crispy pancake stuffed with pork and shrimp, as well as vegetables. It is also known as a sizzling crepe because of the noise it makes when it is dropped into hot oil. Vietnamese people like to eat these crepes with a dipping sauce.

Iced coffee

Pho is also known as Vietnamese soup.

The ao dai is made up of a long tunic that is close-fitted to the body, and wide-legged pants. The ao dai is also uniquely designed depending on the region in Vietnam it's from.

To draw the ao dai, begin with the base of a person.

Add the tunic and the hat.

Lastly, draw on the designs of your tunic! You can choose anything from flowers, to animals, to patterns.

—— Bánh Xèo ——

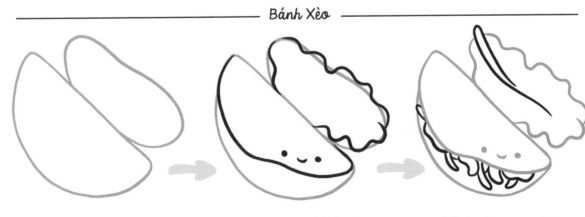

Draw a semicircle for the crepe and a jelly bean for the lettuce.

Continue to fill in the crepe with a top layer, and draw squiggles around the lettuce.

Fill in the crepe with goodies like vegetables and meat!

You know what to do: draw a base with a circle and oval!

Connect the base to the top of the head. Add limbs and triangle ears.

The face of the monkey is two connected ovals.

Finish with a cute face. Make the nose with two little dots.

Lotus flower

The national flower of Vietnam is the lotus, which grows in water.

Draw the base of your person with one arm up to hold the shoulder pole.

Draw a long line for the pole, and add the hat, face, collar, buttons, and feet.

The baskets are like two large teardrops. Add in hair, circles for hands, and footwear.

Dragon fruit

Lettuce

Bananas

Tomato

Shoulder poles are made from bamboo and are used to carry heavy baskets of vegetables, fruit, and flowers.

Add another line to connect each basket to the shoulder pole, then add your details.

Water buffalo

There are lots of water buffalo in Vietnam. They are used to till the fields in the countryside and also for milk.

There are some amazing sand dunes in Vietnam. People like riding over them in special desert bikes.

Desert bikes are made up of many shapes! Draw circles, a triangle, and a rectangle.

Start connecting all the shapes with an outline. Add small lines for the details of the wheels.

Complete the bike with a handle and fun face.

Motorcycles are a common vehicle in Vietnam for transportation and carrying heavy loads about.

Draw a triangle and two circles for the base of the motorcycle . . .

. . . then draw the base of a person sitting on top. Start filling in the structure of the bike.

Add on rectangles to show that the person is carrying many boxes on the back of the bike.

Give your rider hair and a hat, and an extra box to carry on the handlebars.

—— *Pearls* ——

Pearls are found inside oyster shells. They are shiny and usually a creamy white color. Pearls are used in jewelry because they are so pretty.

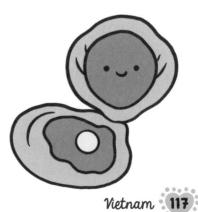

AUSTRALIA

Australia is a huge island country in the Southern Hemisphere. It has lots of amazing beaches, such as Bondi Beach, and also the colorful Great Barrier Reef. Famous cities include Sydney, Melbourne, and Brisbane. Australia is home to some well-known animals too, including kangaroos, koalas, and echidnas.

The Australian flag

Sydney Opera House is one of the world's most famous landmarks. You will also find the incredible Sydney Harbour Bridge and Sydney Botanical Garden in the city.

The thorny devil is a type of lizard found in Australia.

Golden wattle flowers are very fragrant.

Lifeguards in Australia are always ready to rush in to the sea if a swimmer gets into trouble.

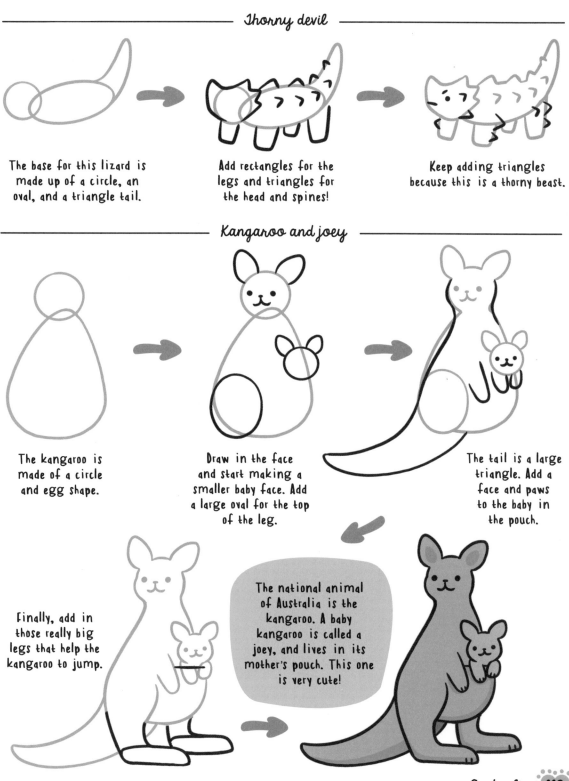

Thorny devil

The base for this lizard is made up of a circle, an oval, and a triangle tail.

Add rectangles for the legs and triangles for the head and spines!

Keep adding triangles because this is a thorny beast.

Kangaroo and joey

The kangaroo is made of a circle and egg shape.

Draw in the face and start making a smaller baby face. Add a large oval for the top of the leg.

The tail is a large triangle. Add a face and paws to the baby in the pouch.

Finally, add in those really big legs that help the kangaroo to jump.

The national animal of Australia is the kangaroo. A baby kangaroo is called a joey, and lives in its mother's pouch. This one is very cute!

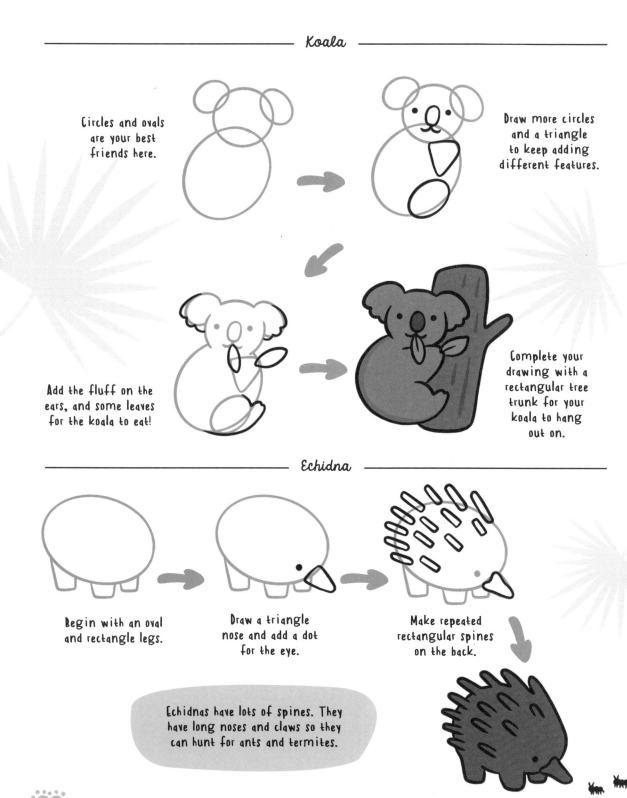

Koala

Circles and ovals are your best friends here.

Draw more circles and a triangle to keep adding different features.

Add the fluff on the ears, and some leaves for the koala to eat!

Complete your drawing with a rectangular tree trunk for your koala to hang out on.

Echidna

Begin with an oval and rectangle legs.

Draw a triangle nose and add a dot for the eye.

Make repeated rectangular spines on the back.

Echidnas have lots of spines. They have long noses and claws so they can hunt for ants and termites.

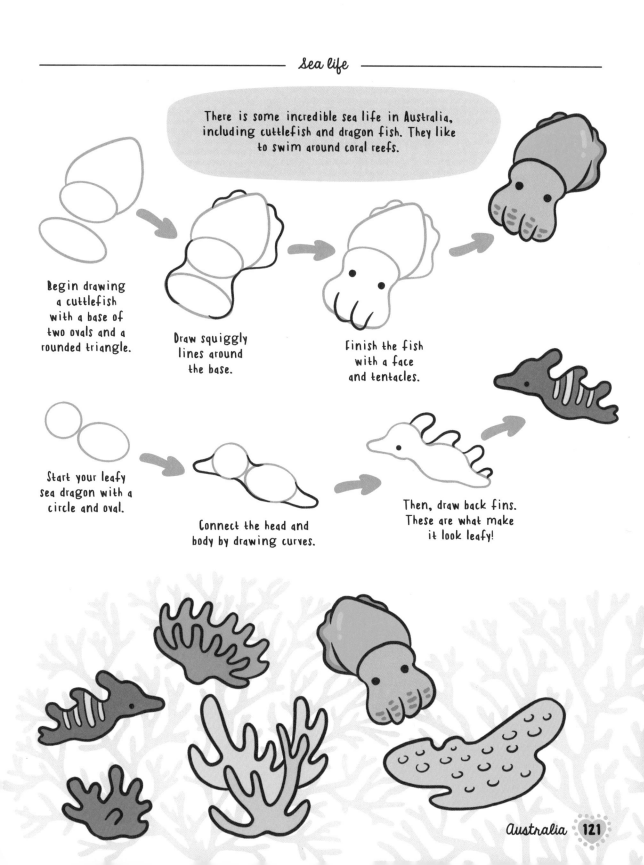

There is some incredible sea life in Australia, including cuttlefish and dragon fish. They like to swim around coral reefs.

Begin drawing a cuttlefish with a base of two ovals and a rounded triangle.

Draw squiggly lines around the base.

Finish the fish with a face and tentacles.

Start your leafy sea dragon with a circle and oval.

Connect the head and body by drawing curves.

Then, draw back fins. These are what make it look leafy!

Australia is well known for its beaches. Lifeguards patrol the beaches to keep them safe.

Start your lifeguard with the base of a person and include one arm and leg.

Add the other arm and leg. The second leg is bent to show the lifeguard is running.

Continue adding details like the hat and surfboard.

Finish the drawing with the details on the clothing and hair.

Beach umbrella

Sun hat

Beach chair

Basket

Lamington

A lamington is a sponge cake with chocolate and desiccated coconut around the outside and cream or jam sandwiched in the middle.

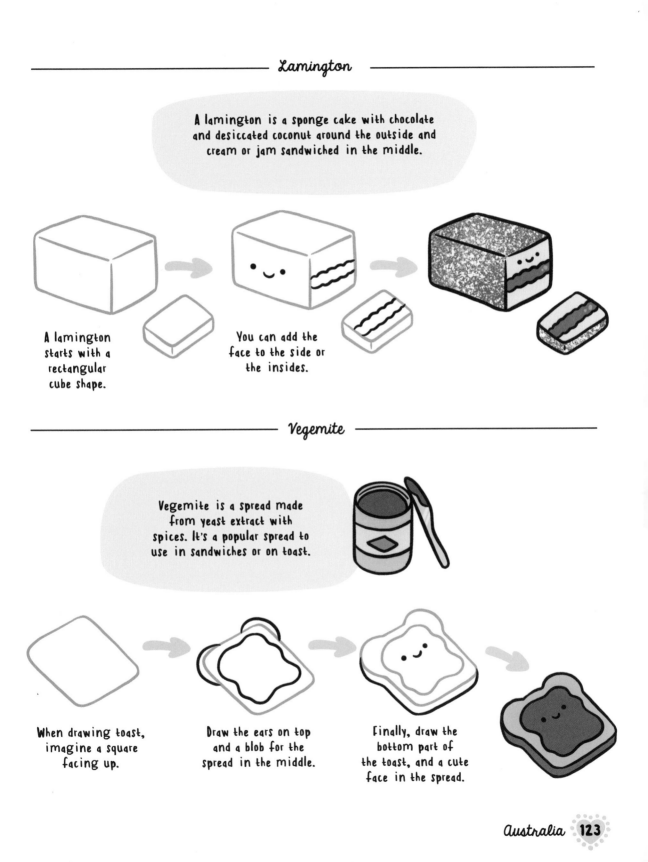

A lamington starts with a rectangular cube shape.

You can add the face to the side or the insides.

Vegemite

Vegemite is a spread made from yeast extract with spices. It's a popular spread to use in sandwiches or on toast.

When drawing toast, imagine a square facing up.

Draw the ears on top and a blob for the spread in the middle.

Finally, draw the bottom part of the toast, and a cute face in the spread.

NEW ZEALAND

The New Zealand flag

New Zealand is near Australia in the Southern Hemisphere. It is made up of two islands: North Island and South Island. The capital city is Wellington. New Zealand's first people are the Maori. You can visit their traditional villages and learn about their customs.

New Zealand is the first country to see the sun rise every day.

One of the nicknames for Auckland, a city on North Island, is the City of Sails, because of all the boats that can be seen on the water there.

There are a lot of sheep in New Zealand.

Manuka honey comes from the nectar of the manuka tree, which is native to New Zealand.

Sailboat

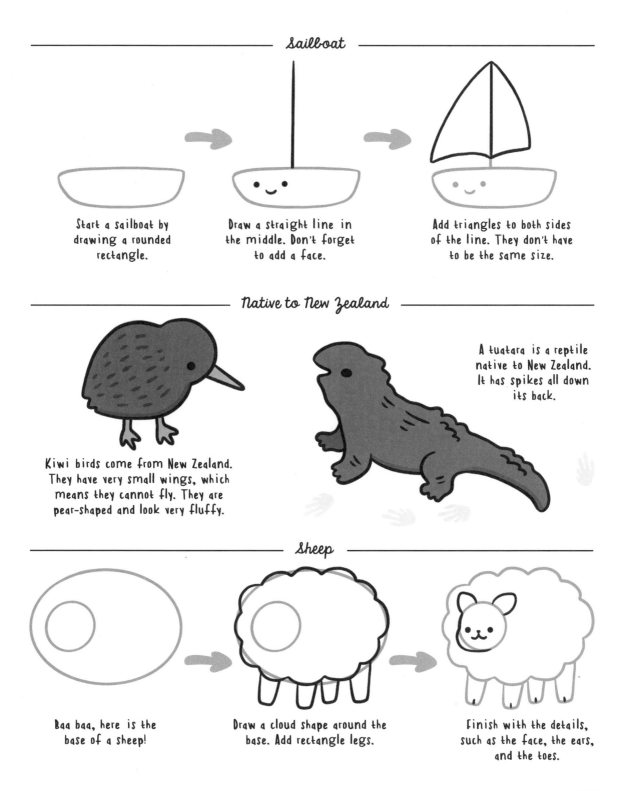

Start a sailboat by drawing a rounded rectangle.

Draw a straight line in the middle. Don't forget to add a face.

Add triangles to both sides of the line. They don't have to be the same size.

Native to New Zealand

Kiwi birds come from New Zealand. They have very small wings, which means they cannot fly. They are pear-shaped and look very fluffy.

A tuatara is a reptile native to New Zealand. It has spikes all down its back.

Sheep

Baa baa, here is the base of a sheep!

Draw a cloud shape around the base. Add rectangle legs.

Finish with the details, such as the face, the ears, and the toes.

Rugby is very popular in New Zealand. The national team is called the All Blacks.

The haka is a special Maori dance. At the beginning of an international rugby match, the All Blacks rugby team perform a haka in the hope that it will intimidate the other team.

Create the base of a person with their arms and legs in a fun dance.

Draw parts of the clothing and the face on top of the base.

Add the hair and patterns to the clothing.

Musical notes show the man is dancing. People performing the haka don't usually look this smiley!

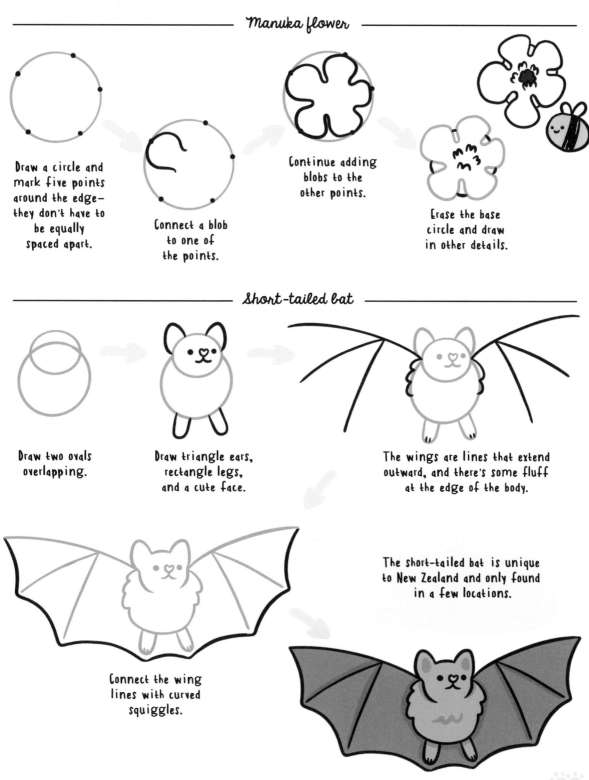

Manuka flower

Draw a circle and mark five points around the edge—they don't have to be equally spaced apart.

Connect a blob to one of the points.

Continue adding blobs to the other points.

Erase the base circle and draw in other details.

Short-tailed bat

Draw two ovals overlapping.

Draw triangle ears, rectangle legs, and a cute face.

The wings are lines that extend outward, and there's some fluff at the edge of the body.

Connect the wing lines with curved squiggles.

The short-tailed bat is unique to New Zealand and only found in a few locations.

CREDITS

Author Acknowledgments

I have to start by thanking the entire publishing team. Thank you for being there with me through all these years, from book one to book five, and helping me bring my sketches to life. I've had the honor of working with such a collaborative and quirky group. These cute books are just as much yours as they are mine.

Picture Credits

Quarto would like to thank the following Shutterstock contributors
for supplying images for inclusion in this book:

SHUTTERSTOCK.COM

Agnieszka Karpinska; Alexiushan; aliaksei kruhlenia; Alona S; ang intaravichian; baoyan; Camp 1994; caramelina; Cat_arch_angel; Christos Georghiou; Egor Shilov; Forgem; GraphicsRF. com; Greens87; Hanna Kh; janista; K.Sorokin; Katika; kleyman; krkt; lazy clouds; Margaret Jone Wollman; Marta Jonina; meow_meow; MuchMania; nikiteev_konstantin; Oleg7799; Seita; shaineast; SimpLine; Solomatina; Tako design; Toltemara; Vector memory; voyata; Wilm Ihlenfeld; Yurkalmmortal; Ziluß; ziviani